MW01490322

THE
VICTORY
JOURNAL

Tanya C. Stokes

WESTBOW
PRESS®
A DIVISION OF THOMAS NELSON
& ZONDERVAN

WestBow Press books may be ordered through booksellers or by contacting:

WestBow Press
A Division of Thomas Nelson & Zondervan
1663 Liberty Drive
Bloomington, IN 47403
www.westbowpress.com
1 (866) 928-1240

ISBN: 978-1-5127-2219-2 (sc)

Library of Congress Control Number: 2015920357

Print information available on the last page.

WestBow Press rev. date: 12/09/2015

Section I

What's Your Aim?

This journal will be best used if you set a specific goal that you would like to achieve. Listed below is an outline of how to set goals.

SMART Goals

A SMART goal involves setting goals that are specific, measurable, attainable, relevant and time based. Every goal should be very clear and concise.

S = Specific

Your goal must clearly state what is to be achieved and when you would like to accomplish it. Be as specific as possible when writing out your goal. For instance, if your goal is to lose weight, you would need to state it in a way that describes exactly what you want to do. Notice the goal below. Rather than stating a goal of losing an undetermined amount of weight, it states how much weight to be lost and the goal of getting back into a particular size.

> Example: I would like to lose 50 pounds and get back into a size 10

M = Measurable

If your goal is not measurable, then it is not possible to know whether you are making progress toward successful completion of your goal. In order to have measurable goals there is usually a number involved - dollars, days, times per week, weight. When you create a goal that is measurable, it's easy to determine when you are getting closer or if you have reached your goal. A measurable goal will usually answer questions such as:

- How much?
- How many?
- How often?
- On what days?
- How will I know when it is accomplished?

Example: I want to save $1000 by the end of the calendar year (December 31st) and I will save $84 per month to accomplish this goal.

A = Attainable

When you set your goals, you must make sure they are attainable. If you set goals that are out of achievable range within the timeframe you desire to achieve them, then you are highly unlikely to reach success. Make sure you evaluate the date by which you want to achieve your goal against the goal itself to ensure you will reach completion.

R = Relevant

Your goals must be relevant to what you want to achieve in the short-term or long-term. Understanding your personal vision, mission and purpose is critical in this respect. Sometimes it can be tempting to do something because everyone else is doing it or because it sounds good. Stick with goals that are connected to where you are going.

T = Time-Based

Any goal you set must have an end date of completion, even if the date is two years from now. When goals are left open-ended, then there is a great chance that the goal will not be accomplished, and it is like saying, "One day I will get my degree." When you set a specific date for accomplishing your goals, you are then able to put yourself on a daily, monthly or yearly system of action that coincides with what you want to accomplish.

Goal #1:

_____

_____

Goal #2:

_____

_____

Goal #3:

_____

_____

Section II

How Will I Get There?

Please list your strategy for completing your goals. For example, if one of your goals is to lose thirty pounds, your strategy could be doing one hour of cardio exercise five days a week, eliminating sweets and snacks, along with doing weight training three times a week.

Goal #1 Strategy:

_____

_____

_____

Goal #2 Strategy:

_____

_____

_____

Goal #3 Strategy:

_____

_____

_____

Section III

Target Achievement Date

1. Goal #1 Begin Date: _____   End Date: _____

2. Goal #2 Begin Date: _____   End Date: _____

3. Goal #3 Begin Date: _____   End Date: _____

Section IV

Putting it All Together

Goals to Accomplish	Write the Goal! Be Specific!	What is your strategy for accomplishing this goal?	Date: When do you intend for goal to be accomplished?
Goal #1			
Goal #2			
Goal #3			

Section V

Let's Do It!

Now that you have specifically identified your aim, outlined a strategy and target achievement date, it's time to do it! You can begin to take one goal at a time and journal your journey of success. This journal will help you discover the mysteries of success. You will learn things about yourself and what challenges that you may not have known were blocking your progress. You will discover your mindset and ways of thinking that attempt to sabotage your success and much more. Please feel free to discuss your ups and downs in this journal, record your small and large victories and your transformation along the way. I am rooting for you because I believe you are a champion! Enjoy your journey!

Tanya C. Stokes

Printed in the United States
By Bookmasters